DECORATE LIFE :

HOME DÉCOR

CONTENTS

Prepare to be amazed how much this collection of simple-to-create projects can change the entire feel of your home. Now, start Decorating Life.

DECORATE LIFE : HOME DÉCOR

1
PHOTO DÉCOR WALL

TILE NUMBERS

USE CHIPBOARD NUMBERS TO CREATE HIGH-GLOSS FAUX TILES

HOW DO I LOVE THEE . . . BY LONI STEVENS

(TIP)
PLACE PAINTED NUMBERS ON JAR LIDS WHEN POURING
HIGH GLOSS FINISH OVER THEM, ALLOWING EPOXY RESIN
TO DRIP OFF THE SIDES AND THROUGH THE NUMBERS

SHADOW BOX SHELF

CREATE A NEW FACADE USING SMALL, DECORATIVE FRAMES

PHOTO SHELF BY JAYME SHEPHERD

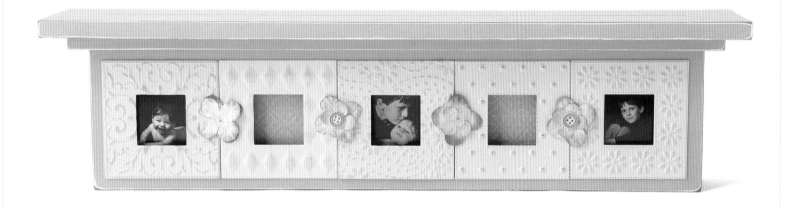

(TIP)

PLACE PICTURES SEVERAL INCHES BEHIND FRAME
OPENING FOR PHOTOGRAPHIC DIMENSION

CLIPBOARD FRAME

EASILY CONVERT TO HOLD A CALENDAR, RECIPE OR NOTEPAD

BEAUTIFUL MOMENTS BY LYNNE MONTGOMERY

(TIP)
WHILE PAINTING, PLACE PIECE OF WAX PAPER
UNDER CLIP TO PREVENT STICKING

WINDOW FRAMES

SHOWCASE PHOTO MATTE ON FRONT SIDE OF GLASS

MIA AND CHLOE BY JENNIFER JENSEN

(TIP)
REPLACE OLD OR CRACKED GLASS WITH NEW
PLEXIGLASS FROM A HARDWARE STORE

HIP TO BE SQUARE

A MODERN TWIST ON THE TRADITIONAL WREATH

GRANDCHILDREN PHOTO WREATH BY MELLETTE BEREZOSKI

If I had known how
wonderful it would
be to have
grandchildren
I'd have had them
first.
-Lois Wyse

(TIP)
PAINT METAL FRAMES TO CREATE A SENSE OF GREENERY

WINDOW TO THE SOUL

TURN AN ABANDONED WINDOW FRAME INTO AN ART CENTER

WINDOW FRAME BULLETIN BOARD BY ERIN TERRELL

[SMILE]

WE ARE NEVER MORE FULLY ALIVE,
MORE COMPLETELY OURSELVES,
OR MORE DEEPLY ENGROSSED IN
ANYTHING THAN WHEN WE ARE

PLAYING

Charles Schaefer

(TIP)

JUXTAPOSE THE WORN WINDOW FRAME WITH SHINY SHEET METAL AND CRISP BLACK AND WHITE PHOTOS

MODERN VINTAGE
OLD MADE NEW

we had the same dreams, locked away, not knowing that our paths would cross someday. And when they finally did, it was as if we had known each other all our lives. And we realized that from the very beginning, we were destined to

LOVE.

(TIP)
FOR A COHESIVE LOOK, LINE INSIDE OF SHADOW
BOX WITH VINTAGE HIP BORDER STICKERS

METAL-RIMMED MATTE
ADD SPARKLE AND DIMENSION WITH MICRO-BEADS

EFFORTLESS BY LONI STEVENS

(TIP)
COVER CHIPBOARD WITH BEADS, SHAKE OFF EXCESS AND
DROP BACK INTO TAG MAKER TO CRIMP METAL RIM SHUT

UPHOLSTERED IN PAPER

TURN AN INEXPENSIVE WOODEN
FRAME INTO A WORK OF ART

BOHO FRAME BY GAIL PIERCE-WATNE

(TIP)

DECOUPAGE PAPER ON A PLAIN FRAME FOR
A DURABLE AND DECORATIVE RESULT

(TIP)
USE PAPER AND TRIMS FROM A SINGLE LINE TO ENSURE COORDINATION

2
PHOTO DÉCOR
TABLE

UPRIGHT ALBUM

CREATE STAND-UP FLIP FRAMES USING
COORDINATING PAPER AND EMBELLISHMENTS

PHOTO FLIP FRAME BY JAYME SHEPHERD

(TIP)
USE DIMENSIONAL ADHESIVES TO MAKE
A SPECIFIC ELEMENT STAND OUT

(TIP)
ADD A RUB-ON SUBTITLE TO COMPLETE A SENTIMENT

RIBBON MATTE

DRESS UP A FRAMED PHOTO WITH A CUSTOMIZED MATTE

H BY JOANNA BOLICK

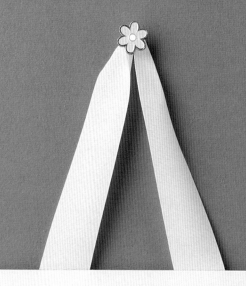

(TIP)

PLACE RIBBON VERTICALLY OR HORIZONTALLY TO COMPLIMENT YOUR PHOTO OR TRY A MIXTURE OF BOTH FOR A PATCHWORK EFFECT

CLIP AND WIRE DISPLAY
USE SEVERAL SHOTS FROM THE SAME PHOTO SESSION

FAMILY TRI-FOLD FRAME BY JAYME SHEPHERD

(TIP)
WHEN COVERING CHIPBOARD LETTERS WITH
PAPER, SIMPLY CUT OUT PAPER, GLUE TO LETTER
AND SAND AWAY EDGES FOR A SMOOTH FINISH

SHADOW BOX SPOTLIGHT

DIVIDE PATTERNED PAPERS INTO SMALL SQUARED BACKGROUNDS

BEAUTIFUL BRIDE SHADOW BOX BY JAYME SHEPHERD

(TIP)

USE RIBBON AND SANDING TO CREATE UNIQUE BORDERS ON PHOTOS

VERTICAL FRAMES

COMBINE METAL AND RIBBON FOR VISUAL TEXTURE

OLIVER BY HILLARY LANDON

(TIP)
PAINTING METAL MESH ADDS A SOFTER, CUSTOM APPEARANCE

ENCIRCLED SNAPSHOTS

MIX AND MATCH PAPER COLORS AND TEXTURES

PHOTO WREATH BY GAIL PIERCE-WATNE

(TIP)

MATCH PAPERS AND TRIMS BY MAKING SELECTIONS FROM THE SAME
PAPER LINE, THEN MIX IT UP USING PATTERNS AND TEXTURES

WARMEST WISHES

SIGNAGE AND PHOTOS MAKE ANY ACCESSORY PERSONAL

PHOTO CANDLE TRIO BY MELLETTE BEREZOSKI

discover

reflect

enjoy

(TIP)

SECURE OBJECTS TO CANDLES USING THUMBTACKS

BOXED IN

DISPLAY A FAVORITE PHOTO OR HOUSE
A TREASURE IN EMBELLISHED BOXES

GOALS 2006 BY LYNNE MONTGOMERY

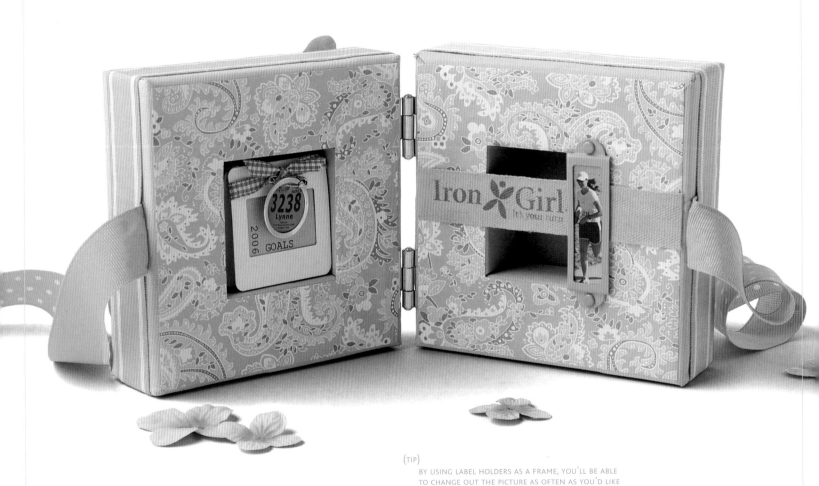

(TIP)

BY USING LABEL HOLDERS AS A FRAME, YOU'LL BE ABLE
TO CHANGE OUT THE PICTURE AS OFTEN AS YOU'D LIKE

SUSPENDED REALITY

THREAD RIBBON THROUGH LIGHTWEIGHT FRAMES FOR VERTICAL DISPLAY

HANGING FRAMES BY GAIL PIERCE-WATNE

(TIP)
KEEP COLORS SUBTLE SO YOUR PHOTOS
REMAIN THE MAIN ATTRACTION

MAGNETIC MEMORABILIA
PHOTO FRAME AND NOTE BOARD COMBINED
SISTERS BY LYNNE MONTGOMERY

(TIP)
CUT SEVERAL METAL PIECES AT A TIME
AND SET ASIDE FOR QUICK GIFTS

GO SHEER

SEE-THROUGH FRAMES MAKE
ONE-OF-A-KIND COASTERS

GLASS PHOTO COASTERS BY MELLETTE BEREZOSKI

(TIP)
GLASS CAN BE CUT TO SIZE AND FINISHED AT MOST
HARDWARE OR HOME IMPROVEMENT STORES

3
DÉCOR ACCENTS
WALL

MIRRORED MEMORIES

ATTACH SMALL FRAMES USING STRONG, DOUBLE-SIDED TAPE

MONOGRAM MIRROR BY MAGGIE HOLMES

(TIP)
PHOTOS AND EMBELLISHMENTS CAN
EASILY BE UPDATED OVER TIME

ORNAMENTAL CANVAS
USE PAINT AND RIBBON TO DECORATE A BLANK CANVAS

HISTORY *BY* LONI STEVENS

history. preserving the past. creating the future. a legacy of love.

(TIP)
GIVE VINTAGE TRIM NEW LIFE BY INCORPORATING
IT INTO A MODERN, CLEAN DESIGN

~ ONCE YOU MAKE A DECISION THE UNIVERSE CONSPIRES TO MAKE IT HAPPEN.
Ralph Waldo Emerson

(TIP)

RUB-ONS STICK WELL TO MIRRORS,
BUT CAN EASILY BE SWAPPED FOR
NEW QUOTES

EMOTION EMBELLISHED

SHOW AND SAY EXACTLY WHAT YOU'RE FEELING BY COMBINING LETTERS AND PHOTOS

BOHO LOVE BY GAIL PIERCE-WATNE

(TIP)
COVER CHIPBOARD LETTERS WITH YOUR FAVORITE PAPER FOR A CUSTOMIZED LOOK

TIME PIECE

PAINT AND SAND METAL TIN FRAMES FOR A CUSTOMIZED CLOCK

PHOTO CLOCK BY LONI STEVENS

(TIP)

TRY USING PICTURES THAT ILLUSTRATE THE PASSAGE OF TIME

(TIP)
INSTEAD OF SANDING TO ACHIEVE VINTAGE LOOK,
TRY SCRAPING EDGES WITH A RAZOR BLADE

GET HOOKED

CREATE ORNATE OPENINGS FOR HOOKS USING METAL FRAMES

EVERYTHING HOOKS BY JENNIFER JENSEN

(TIP) MOST LUMBERYARDS WILL CUT
WOOD INTO THE SIZE YOU NEED
FOR LITTLE OR NO COST

DOOR MONOGRAM

KID-FRIENDLY PROJECT WITH VINTAGE APPEAL

MONOGRAM DOOR HANGER BY KRIS STANGER

(TIP)

CHOOSE YOUR MONOGRAM STICKER FIRST,
THEN SELECT A CONTRASTING PAINT COLOR
FOR THE PLAQUE

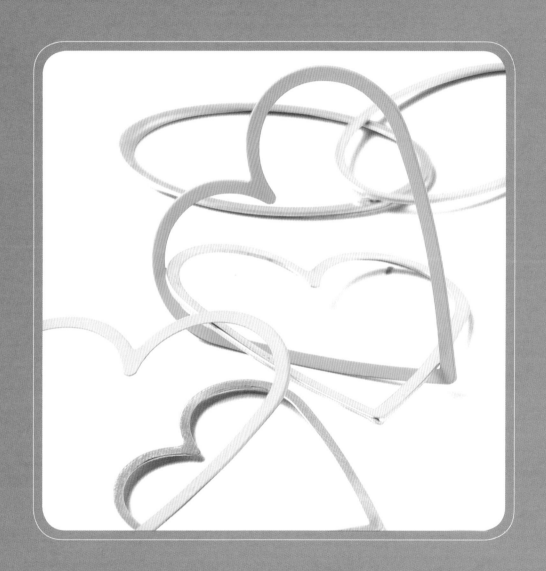

4
DÉCOR ACCENTS
TABLE

SERVING SET

CREATE AN INTERESTING BACKGROUND USING
COORDINATED RIBBON, PAPER AND EMBELLISHMENTS

PHOTO TRAY BY JAYME SHEPHERD

(TIP)

USE GLITTER TO ADD NEW DIMENSION TO METAL LETTERS

LUNCHBOX TIN

ADD PATTERNS USING SPRAY PAINT AND PAGE REINFORCERS

LET THE JOURNEY BEGIN BY LONI STEVENS

(TIP)

USE LOW-TACK PAINTER'S TAPE TO KEEP EDGES CLEAN

RIBBONS AND TRIMS

COMBINE DECORATIVE BANDS TO CUSTOMIZE A PLAIN LAMPSHADE

RIBBON LAMP SHADE BY MARGIE ROMNEY-ASLETT

(TIP) MIX DIFFERENT MATERIALS, STYLES AND TEXTURES OF RIBBON

QUICK CANDLES
USE BRADS AND SNAPS FOR AN EASY, UNIQUE LOOK

BRAD EMBELLISHED CANDLES BY LYNNE MONTGOMERY

(TIP)
DON'T PLACE BRADS TOO CLOSE TO TOP
RIM OR BOTTOM EDGE OF YOUR CANDLE,
WHICH MAY CAUSE BREAKAGE

HIP HEAT

TIE OR GLUE RIBBONS AROUND CANDLE
FOR A DESIGNER CENTERPIECE

RED VH CANDLES BY AUDRE MATHIS

(TIP)

USE METAL GLUE TO ADHERE RIBBONS
TO CANDLE FOR A STRONG HOLD AND
FAST DRYING TIME

BUTTON CLOCK
UTILIZE DECORATIVE ACCENTS

FRAMED BUTTON CLOCK BY JENNIFER JENSEN

(TIP)
SPRAY PAINT CLOCK HANDS TO COORDINATE WITH FRAME AND BUTTONS

CITATION TRANSFER

DECORATE YOUR HOME WITH WORDS

CHERISH ALL YOUR HAPPY MOMENTS BY LONI STEVENS

Cherish all your **happy** moments. They make a fine **cushion** for old age. CHRISTOPHER MORLEY

(TIP) FOLLOW PACKAGE INSTRUCTIONS FOR INK-JET TRANSFER, REMEMBERING TO REVERSE TEXT

CLEVER COASTERS

PERSONALIZE TABLE SETTINGS WITH COASTERS
FEATURING PHOTOS OF GUESTS

FRAMED PHOTO COASTERS BY LYNNE MONTGOMERY

(TIP)
HAVE EDGES OF GLASS SANDED OR FINISHED
TO PREVENT CUTS WHILE HANDLING COASTERS

DECKED OUT SPHERES

USE SCRAPBOOK EMBELLISHMENTS FOR HOME DÉCOR

DECORATIVE BALLS TRIO BY MELLETTE BEREZOSKI

(TIP)

LOOK FOR WOODEN OR PAPIER-MÂCHÉ BALLS AT
CRAFT, HOME IMPROVEMENT OR ANTIQUE SHOPS

GREETINGS AND SALUTATIONS
MONOGRAM ALPHABETS AND CIRCLE CLIPS MAKE CARD DISPLAY A CINCH

GREETINGS CARD HOLDER BY MELLETTE BEREZOSKI

(TIP)
TRY ATTACHING LETTERS TO A PLEXI-GLASS BACKGROUND

GLASS VASE

ADD SUBTLE PATTERNS FOR A DRAMATIC EFFECT

EVERYTHING GROWS WITH LOVE BY LONI STEVENS

[everything grows with love.]

(TIP)
COVER INSIDE OF VASE WITH TISSUES
TO PROTECT FROM STICKY SPRAY

FOAM-STAMPED HOLDER
ANTIQUE AND DISTRESS WOOD

DISTRESSED CANDLE HOLDER BY KRIS STANGER

(TIP)
DON'T WORRY ABOUT BEING TOO CAREFUL WHILE
STAMPING THIS PROJECT; ROUGHING IT UP IS THE GOAL

5
ENTERTAINING

WHEN YOU WISH

DECORATIVE JARS HOUSE MAKE AND TAKE MESSAGES

WISHING JARS BY MELLETTE BEREZOSKI

(TIP)
WRAP PAPER STRIPS TIGHTLY AROUND PENCIL TO COIL

SHOWER BOUQUET

CREATE RIBBON ROSES FOR TABLE DECORATIONS

SHOWER INVITATION BY GAIL PIERCE-WATNE

(TIP)
PULL WIRE FROM WIRED RIBBON TO GATHER INTO A PERFECT ROSEBUD

CONFIGURED GLASS
ADD SEMI-TRANSPARENT PATTERNS USING GLASS FROSTING SPRAY

DECORATIVE GLASSES BY LONI STEVENS

(TIP)
USE PADDLE PUNCHES TO CREATE MASKS OUT OF
LOW-TACK TAPE OR CLEAR WINDOW DECALS

WELCOME, GUESTS

MAKE A BEDSIDE SIGN-IN BOOK FOR OVERNIGHT VISITORS

OUR FRIENDS, OUR GUESTS BY JENNIFER JENSEN

(TIP)
SET ASIDE SPACE FOR GUESTS TO WRITE A MEMORY
AND LEAVE A DISPOSABLE CAMERA SO PHOTO CAN
LATER BE PLACED NEXT TO COMMENTS

TAKE A SEAT

TAILOR PLACE CARDS TO INDIVIDUAL GUESTS

A CELEBRATION OF FAMILY BY JULIE TURNER

(TIP)
WIPE FRAME AND BRADS WITH WHITE
ACRYLIC PAINT FOR A VINTAGE LOOK

FAMILY GATHERING

STIR UP MEMORIES BY COMBINING VINTAGE PAPER WITH FAMILY PHOTOS

A CELEBRATION OF FAMILY BY JULIE TURNER

(TIP)

CUSTOMIZE EACH INVITATION WITH A PHOTO THAT
HAS SENTIMENTAL MEANING FOR THE RECIPIENT

INVITING FAVORS
CONVERT A SMALL TIN INTO AN ORIGINAL PARTY GIFT

IT'S A PARTY BY AUDRE MATHIS

What   Birthday Party for Jen!

when   Saturday, March 14th

where   283 Point St.

Rsvp   801.598.0430

{ me *and* the girls }

Jen

(TIP)
SOAK PAPER PIECES IN WATER BEFORE
ADHERING TO TIN WITH MOD PODGE

FLOWER STAMPS

EMBOSS PETALS FOR ADDED DEPTH AND TEXTURE

JOIN US BY LONI STEVENS

(TIP)
PLACE VELLUM OVER A BOLD PATTERN FOR A SOFT, SUBTLE LOOK

NUMERICAL ORDER
UNIFY PLACE SETTINGS BY REPEATING ELEMENTS

SWEET 16 PLACE SETTING BY MELLETTE BEREZOSKI

(TIP)
COLOR, CIRCLES AND NUMBERS
BRING THIS PARTY TOGETHER

(TIP)
MAKE IT 'ALL GIRL' WITH SCALLOPED EDGES, GEMS AND RIBBON

PAPER POCKETS

SIGN SENTIMENTS IN YOUR OWN PERSONAL SPACE

SWEET 16 GUEST BOOK BY MELLETTE BEREZOSKI

(TIP)

ADD RIBBONS TO TOP OF TAGS FOR EASY ACCESS

PRICELESS PACKAGE
PHOTOS AND PATTERNED PAPER TURN
AN ORDINARY BOX INTO A CHERISHED GIFT

FRIENDSHIP FAVOR BOXES BY MELLETTE BEREZOSKI

(TIP)

PARTY FAVOR IDEAS FOR BOX INCLUDE:
SMALL TOYS AND CANDY FOR YOUNG CHILDREN
LIP GLOSS AND NAIL POLISH FOR TEENS
JEWELRY AND GIFT CARDS FOR ADULTS

6
STORAGE &
ORGANIZATION

PHOTO STORAGE

FILE FOLDERS BECOME STITCHED STORAGE POCKETS

FILE FOLDERS PHOTO STORAGE BY MAGGIE HOLMES

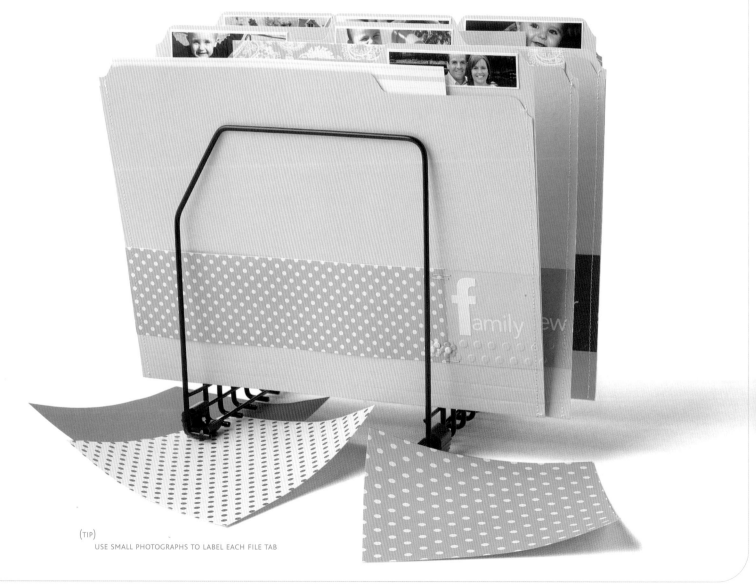

(TIP)

USE SMALL PHOTOGRAPHS TO LABEL EACH FILE TAB

COMBINE FAVORITE PHOTOS AND EMBELLISHMENTS FOR DISPLAY

SHADOW BOX BY MARGIE ROMNEY-ASLETT

GIGGLE

1. *a giddy laughter*
2. **laughter in a silly or nervous manner**
3. often accompanying secrets among young girls

(TIP)

TRACE WINDOWS ONTO BACKING OF PROJECT
TO SERVE AS PHOTO TEMPLATES

TAGGED JARS

STORE AND ORGANIZE IN STYLE

EMBELLISHMENT JARS BY GAIL PIERCE-WATNE

(TIP)
USE MAKING MEMORIES' TAG MAKER
TO CREATE CUSTOMIZED TAGS

EMBELLISHED BOXES

DECORATE PRE-COVERED CONTAINERS
FOR QUICK, IMPRESSIVE PROJECTS

VINTAGE PAPER BOXES BY JAYME SHEPHERD

(TIP)

TRY METAL FRAMES TO FINISH OFF
SMALLER BOX TOP

STACKED RIBBONS

CREATE A BEAUTIFUL DISPLAY AND ORGANIZE ALL AT ONCE

RIBBON RACK BY SKYLAR NIELSEN

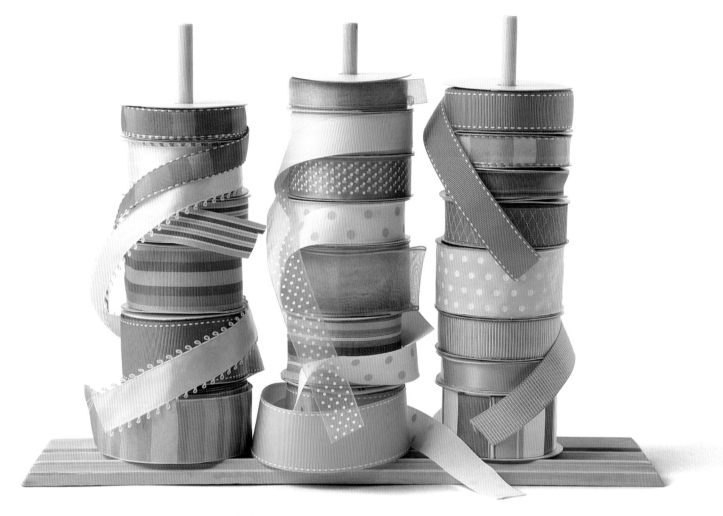

(TIP)
USE EXTRA MOLDING STRIPS AND WOODEN DOWELS

TIED UP IN BOWS

USE WHAT'S INSIDE TO DECORATE THE OUTSIDE

RIBBON JARS BY GAIL PIERCE-WATNE

(TIP)

SEPARATING RIBBON ACCORDING TO
COLOR ADD FUNCTIONAL FLAIR

MODULAR DIVIDES
USE PAPER AND TRIMS TO SEPARATE AND ORGANIZE
EMBELLISHED MOS BY JIHAE KWON

(TIP)
SYSTEMATIZE BY COLOR OR BY THEME

COVER AND CATALOG
STITCHED CD LABELS, PARTITIONS AND MORE

PHOTO CD BOX BY KRIS STANGER

(TIP) CUSTOMIZE A SET OF DIVIDERS FOR JUST ABOUT ANY PROJECT OR GIVE A SET AWAY AS A GIFT

SHELF IT

MADE TO ORDER SHELVES FOR
YOUR SCRAPBOOK ACCESSORIES

SCRAPBOOK STORAGE SHELF BY ERIN TERRELL

(TIP)

LET PAINT, PAPER AND A DISTRESSING
KIT CREATE CUSTOMIZED STORAGE FOR
YOUR SCRAPBOOKING EMBELLISHMENTS

RIBBON WRAPS

STRIPS OF RIBBON TAKE TINS FROM BORING TO BEAUTIFUL

RIBBON CONTAINERS BY ERIN TERRELL

(TIP)

MAKING MEMORIES' RIBBON IS THE PERFECT WIDTH
FOR DECORATING THESE 4 AND 6 OZ. TINS

7
CREATIVE SPACE

INSTANT ART

FRAME AND LABEL IDEA BOOK PHOTOS

ART FRAMES BY ERIN TERRELL

CREATE
TO
LIVE

(TIP) CUSTOM MATTES AND IDEA BOOK PHOTOS CREATE BEAUTIFUL WALL ART

DOUBLE DUTY

POTTING TINS BECOME BOTH BOOKENDS AND STORAGE BINS

PEN HOLDER BOOKENDS BY MELLETTE BEREZOSKI

(TIP)

STABILIZE PENS AND PENCILS BY FILLING TINS HALF WAY WITH PINTO BEANS

BOX SET

INCORPORATE COLOR, BEAUTY AND FUNCTION
WITH THESE SIMPLE, YET UNIQUE STORAGE BOXES

SCRAP ROOM BOXES BY SHERELLE CHRISTENSEN

(TIP)
ADD PAPER AND EMBELLISHMENTS TO EXISTING PAPIER-MÂCHÉ
ITEMS FOR ELEGANT DÉCOR AND STORAGE

SPARKLING SCRIPT

MIX TWO DIFFERENT MATERIALS FOR A DISTINCTIVE EFFECT

SHIMMERED ALPHA BY MARGIE ROMNEY-ASLETT

(TIP)
COMBINE TWO TEXTURES OF GLITTER
FOR COMPLETE COVERAGE

WOODEN MONOGRAM

ADD TEXT USING LETTER STICKERS AS A PAINTING MASK

ART DOESN'T HAVE TO BE PERFECT BY LONI STEVENS

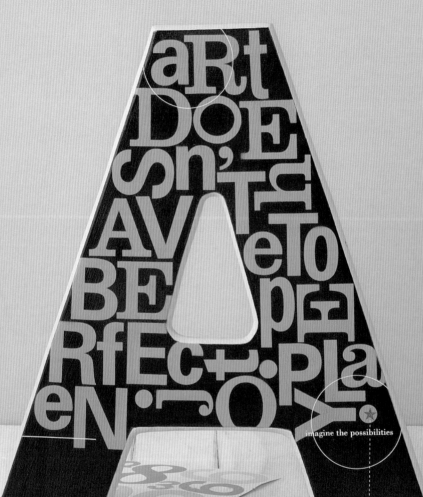

(TIP) ONCE LETTER STICKERS ARE ADHERED, APPLY PAINT IN
THIN LAYERS TO PREVENT IT FROM BLEEDING THROUGH

(TIP)

CHOOSE COLORS THAT WILL COMPLIMENT YOUR ROOM DÉCOR

ALTERED LAMP

PETALS AND DECORATIVE BRADS
QUICKLY TRANSFORM

WHITE LAMP BY LYNNE MONTGOMERY

(TIP)

ADD PETALS TO TOP EDGE OF LAMP
OR COVER THE ENTIRE SHADE

VERTICAL ELEGANCE
KEEP YOUR TREASURES TIDY
HANGING BUCKET BY KRIS STANGER

(TIP)
FILL WITH ANYTHING FROM BUTTONS TO
RIBBONS OR GIVE AWAY AS A UNIQUE GIFT

CUSTOMIZED TAGS

STRING TAGS TOGETHER FOR PLAYFUL ROOM DIVIDERS

JILLIAN'S WORLD BY JULIE TURNER

(TIP)

EACH STRAND OF TAGS HAS A DIFFERENT PERSONALIZED
PHOTO THEME, SUCH AS FRIENDS, BALLET, SCHOOL AND MORE

DECORATIVE DISH

SWEET SENTIMENTS WHILE SERVING SWEETS

SWEET TREATS BY ERIN TERRELL

(TIP)

USE RUB-ON LETTERS TO JAZZ UP AN ORDINARY BOWL

PHOTOS³

DRESS UP AN ORDINARY PAPIER-MÂCHÉ BOX

PHOTO CUBE BY ERIN TERRELL

(TIP)
THIS BOX SERVES TWO PURPOSES; IT SHOWCASES BELOVED PHOTOS,
BUT ALSO ACTS AS STORAGE FOR 6" X 6" MINI ALBUMS

(TIP)
USE BULLDOG CLIPS ALONG BOTTOM SECTIONS
TO DISPLAY PHOTOS, A CALENDAR AND MORE

8
KIDS DÉCOR

WOODEN LETTERS
COVER IN PAPER THAT MATCHES CHILD'S ROOM
ABC CHILDREN'S ROOM BORDER BY JAYME SHEPHERD

(TIP)
HELP CHILD LEARN ABC'S BY PLACING A PICTURE THAT
COORDINATES WITH EACH LETTER; 'D' FOR DADDY

(TIP)
APPLY MOD PODGE OVER PAINT, SEALING
AND ADDING SHINE TO BUCKETS

HANG OUT

SPELL OUT YOUR CHILD'S NAME FOR A UNIQUE DOOR HANGER

KID'S DOOR HANGER BY AUDRE MATHIS

(TIP)
USE THE NEGATIVE SHAPE OF A LETTER AS A PHOTO FRAME

(TIP)

EMBELLISH THE BOARD'S FRAME TO MATCH YOUR DÉCOR

CONNECTED CHIPBOARD
USE RIBBON TO CONNECT SIMPLE CHIPBOARD FRAMES FOR A BEAUTIFUL HANGING DISPLAY

HANGING PHOTO FRAMES BY SHERELLE CHRISTENSEN

(TIP)
ACCENT ANY ROOM IN YOUR HOME WITH
THESE INEXPENSIVE, PAPER-COVERED FRAMES

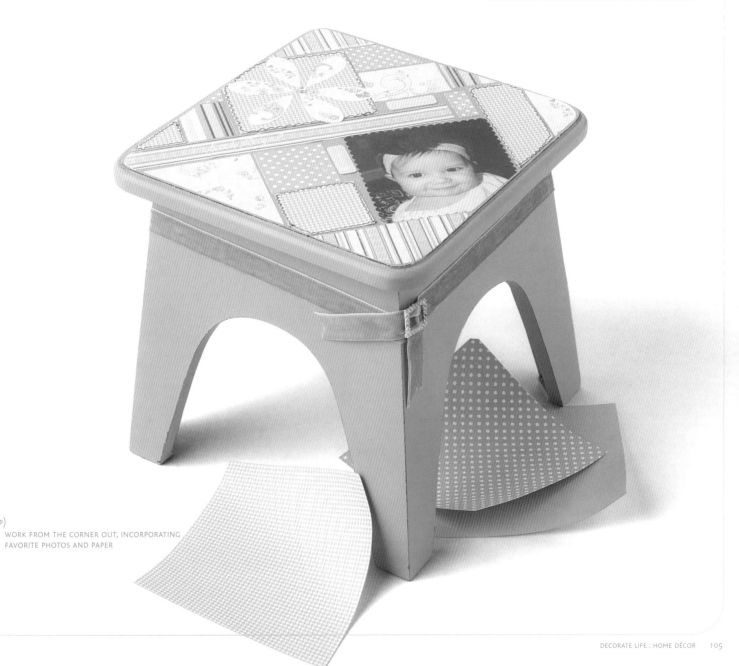

(TIP) WORK FROM THE CORNER OUT, INCORPORATING FAVORITE PHOTOS AND PAPER

GO, TEAM
JERSEY BECOMES KEEPSAKE PILLOW

KIDS PENDANT PILLOW BY JENNIFER JENSEN

(TIP)
LET JERSEY NUMBERS BECOME THE CANVAS FOR
AN IRON-ON PHOTO OF CHILD PLAYING SPORT

GROW UP

FOAM STAMPS AND ACRYLIC PAINTS CREATE CHILDREN'S GROWTH CHART

UP, UP, UP! BY JENNIFER JENSEN

(TIP)

CANVAS FABRIC WORKS AS A GREAT BACKGROUND
FOR PAINT AND RUB-ONS AND CAN ALSO BE DYED
TO MATCH ROOM OR WALL COLR

OLD-TIME TRIO

WALL DÉCOR WITH VINTAGE APPEAL

KEEPSAKE FRAMES BY KRIS STANGER

(TIP)
APPLY A LAYER OF MOD PODGE TO PAPER
FLOWERS FOR SHINE AND DURABILITY

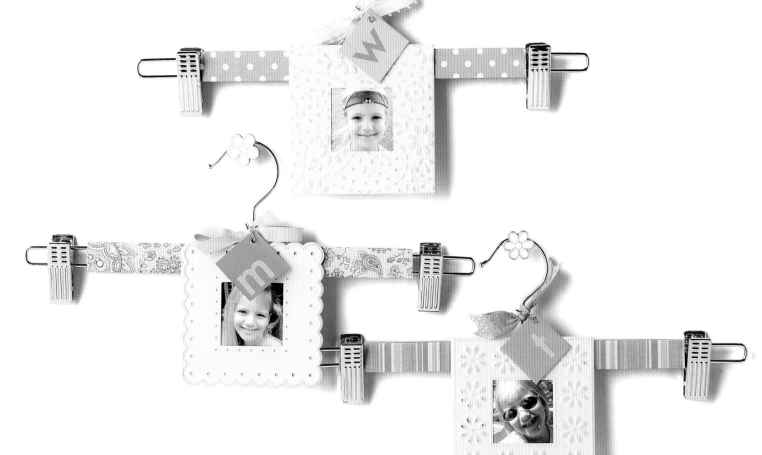

DAILY PLANNER
GAMEBOARD ALPHAS MARK DAYS OF
THE WEEK FOR ORGANIZATION
WEEKDAY PHOTO HANGERS BY MELLETTE BEREZOSKI

(TIP)

HANGERS CAN BE USED TO ORGANIZE CLOTHES FOR THE SCHOOL
WEEK OR CAN BE HUNG ON THE WALL TO HOLD HOMEWORK,
FORMS, NOTES FROM MOM AND MORE

PERSONALITY PANELS

CAPTURE YOUR CHILD'S CHARACTER TRAITS

ALTERED MOS BY MARGIE ROMNEY-ASLETT

(TIP)

USE AN OLD PAIR OF JEANS AS AN EMBELLISHMENT

RIBBON WREATH

COMBINE DIFFERENT COLORS
OF POLKA DOT RIBBON

RIBBON WREATH BY ELENI KARAHALIOS

(TIP)
TO PREVENT CRUSHING, USE UNWIRED RIBBON

9
BOOK END

PAGE 10 LONI STEVENS

HOW DO I LOVE THEE . . .

1. Paint chipboard numbers
2. Pour high gloss finish over numbers and let dry
3. Back each number with brown corduroy material
4. Cut a piece of chipboard to serve as backing for numbers
5. Add photo to center
6. Type journaling strip in Microsoft Word, print on glossy photo paper and adhere over numbers
7. Add ribbon brad to center of flower and set on journaling strip

Jigsaw numbers (poolside), ribbon brad, scrapbook colors acrylic paint and blossoms (wildflower): Making Memories

Acrylic paint: Delta Technical Coatings

Computer font: Quick type

High gloss finish: EnviroTex Lite, Environmental Technology, Inc.

Other: corduroy material

PAGE 11 JAYME SHEPHERD

PHOTO SHELF

1. Paint shelf and sand edges for an antiqued look
2. Remove back of shelf, inner box and glass from shadow box
3. Adhere metal frames to front of shadow box opening
4. Cover inner box with paper
5. Align photos with a few frame openings and adhere to inner box
6. Layer paper flowers with button as center and adhere to frame intersections

Vintage hip frames and buttons (paisley), boho chic paper (lauren), scrapbook colors acrylic paint (shopping bag), blossoms and sandpaper: Making Memories

Shadow box shelf: Provo Craft

PAGE 12 LYNNE MONTGOMERY

BEAUTIFUL MOMENTS

1. Paint metal clip and bolt heads a solid color and let dry completely
2. Choose and arrange decorative papers, stamp if desired and decoupage onto clipboard
3. Age metal clip and bolt heads with brown and black inks and set with sealer

4. Drill holes for bolt placement upon which glass will rest
5. Place photo on board, then cover and secure sheet of glass under clip with bottom edge resting on bolts
6. Embellish with ribbons, rub-ons and more

Vintage hip paper, trims and findings, eyelet letters classic color, jump rings, rub-ons, scrapbook colors acrylic paint kit and distressing kit: Making Memories

Rubber stamp: Hampton Art Stamps

Decoupage and collage gel: API'S Crafter's Pick

PAGE 13 JENNIFER JENSEN

MIA AND CHLOE

1. Place mini glue dots around outer, front edge of photos, center and adhere to back of glass pane
2. Glue buttons around perimeter of photos, adding a rhinestone sticker center to some
3. Apply foam heart stamps onto middle pane
4. Add sticker letters around perimeter of photo
5. Add rhinestones and glue down ribbon and ric rac
6. Tie strands of ribbon to hinge, located on outer edge of window

Vintage hip buttons, foam stamps, gem stickers, eyelet charms (heart), scrapbook colors acrylic paint, alphabet stickers, trims and paper: Making Memories

Other: buttons and old window

PAGE 14 MELLETTE BEREZOSKI

GRANDCHILDREN PHOTO WREATH

1. Paint vintage hip frames, let dry and sand gently with sanding block
2. Cut a 12¾" x 12¾" piece of foam core with a 4⅝" x 4⅝" opening in the center
3. Trim photos to 4¼" x 4¼", then back each with chipboard for stability
4. Attach patterned paper and quote behind painted frames
5. Attach photos and frames to foam core board
6. Add embellishments
7. Attach empty frame (remove glass and backing) to back of wreath for easy wall hanging

Vintage hip frames, trims and paper, scrapbook colors acrylic paint, petals, crystal buckle, photo anchor, crystal brads, gem stickers, buttons and distressing kit: Making Memories

Chipboard: Big Art Brand

Other: foam core board and wood frame

PAGE 15 ERIN TERRELL

WINDOW FRAME BULLETIN BOARD

1. Cut sheet metal to fit first panel and have glass cut to fit second panel
2. Cover board material with fabric and attach using spray adhesive for two bottom panels
3. Create and hang magnets on sheet metal panel
4. Use rub-ons, fabric, ribbon and more to decorate glass section
5. Add paper, ribbon, mini frames, chipboard and rub-ons to decorate bulletin board panels
6. Use push pins to hold artwork or photos in place on bulletin boards
7. Easily swap out photos, paper and ribbons over time to change the look of the board

Vintage hip trims (brooke), frames (dot and flower), trinkets (gracen and paisley) and paper (paisley), rub-ons alphabet (hudson and heidi), chipboard alphabet (poolside), push pin variety pack 3 (heart pin) and magnetic bulldog clips: Making Memories

Glue dots: Glue Dots International

Spray adhesive: Krylon

PAGE 16 MELLETTE BEREZOSKI

LOVE SHADOW BOX

1. Attach vintage hip border stickers to inside edges of shadow box
2. Cut a 4¼" x 12" piece of tan textured cardstock and machine stitch diamond pattern
3. Print journaling onto cardstock and attach to bottom of shadow box
4. Attach ribbon, ribbon attachments, trims and flowers along top edge of cardstock
5. Apply gameboard alphabet, rub-ons images and crystal brad below journaling
6. Attach vintage door plates

Vintage hip border stickers (gracen) and trims, textured cardstock, gameboard alphabet (sadie), rub-ons images, ribbon attachments and crystal brads: Making Memories

Shadow box: Hobby Lobby

Other: vintage door plates

PAGE 17 LONI STEVENS

EFFORTLESS

1. Cut circle inserts out of chipboard to fit metal rimmed tags
2. Paint each chipboard circle
3. Cover select circles with double-sided adhesive and pour on micro-beads
4. Adhere tags to photo matte around opening
5. Set crystal brads over select tags
6. Add text over photo using Photoshop

Crystal brads, metal rimmed tags, tag maker and scrapbook colors acrylic paint: Making Memories

Computer fonts: Nilland and Quick Type

Double-sided adhesive tape and micro-beads: Art Accentz, Provo Craft

PAGE 18 GAIL PIERCE-WATNE

BOHO FRAME

1. Choose wooden frame with smooth surface
2. Cut paper to wrap around frame, covering front, side and inner lip (or apply strips of paper for random look)
3. Moisten paper by dipping briefly in water
4. Apply decoupage to small areas of frame and wrap paper
5. Apply decoupage over entire surface
6. Attach brad and ribbon as embellishments

Boho chic paper and trims and brads: Making Memories

Wooden frame: Target

PAGE 19 MARGIE ROMNEY-ASLETT

WALL WORD HOME

1. Buy wooden letters or chipboard alphabet
2. Select paper trims
3. Trace alpha onto paper, then cut out
4. Adhere paper alpha to chipboard alphabet
5. Embellish

Vintage hip paper (gracen), trims, buttons and trinkets: Making Memories

Wood letters: Pottery Barn

Office clips: Office Depot

Other: adhesive and Plaid Mod Podge

PAGE 22 JAYME SHEPHERD

PHOTO FLIP FRAME

1. Select background paper and cut piece for middle section of cover
2. Sand edges
3. Add photo to large die-cut frame and adhere to background
4. Add photo to small die-cut frame and adhere to background using dimensional adhesive squares in each corner
5. Add ephemera stickers
6. Cut small lace piece to finish top of large ephemera sticker, position two brads through lace and adhere to background
7. Wrap gathered ribbon and lace around bottom of frame and adhere on backside of cover

Boho chic paper (lauren), ephemera stickers, brad accents (lauren) and trims (lauren), photo flip frame, vintage hip trims (gracen) and sticky squares: Making Memories

PAGE 23 MELLETTE BEREZOSKI

HOME PHOTO CLOCK

1. Paint thin, beveled edge of wood plaque
2. Decoupage edges with patterned paper and let dry completely
3. Trim and attach photos to front of wood plaque
4. Apply monogram letters and rub-ons alphabet to bottom of photos
5. Drill hole through wood plaque and attach clock kit

Vintage hip paper (paisley), scrapbook colors acrylic paint, monograms, rub-ons alphabet (beach), blossoms and crystal brad: Making Memories

Wood block and clock kit: Walnut Hollow

Other: Plaid Mod Podge

PAGE 24 JOANNA BOLICK

H

1. Remove matte from frame
2. Adhere lengths of ribbon to center sections of matte and wrap ends around back of matte or trim to size
3. Adhere ribbon to longer sides of frame
4. Slip matte back inside frame
5. If desired, add letter sticker to outside of glass

Ribbon card (lavender), ribbon words (family 1), woven ribbon, simply fabulous trims, MM kids trims, vintage hip trims, ribbon glue and all about alphas stickers: Making Memories

PAGE 25 JAYME SHEPHERD

FAMILY TRI-FOLD FRAME

1. Select photos and crop to fit their designated empty space within frame
2. Make photos with patterned paper
3. Create large silk flower centers using ribbon, buttons and pins
4. Fasten photos and letters onto frame clips
5. Display on a wall or table

Boho chic paper and trims (lauren), MM kids paper (ethan and emma) and trims (kate), vintage hip paper (paisley), trinket pins, buttons (paisley) and trims (paisley), simply fabulous gems and buckles: Making Memories

Paper: Anna Griffin

Silk flowers: Michaels

Tri-fold frame: Pottery Barn

Other: vintage ribbon

PAGE 26 JAYME SHEPHERD

BEAUTIFUL BRIDE SHADOW BOX

1. Create shadow box background by cutting paper into small squares
2. Select large image and adhere ribbon to underside of photo as a border
3. Sand edges of smaller photos
4. Add three layers of sticky squares to back of large photo and adhere to background
5. Embellish center of large flower and adhere to background
6. Add layer of sticky squares to small photos and adhere to background

Boho chic paper (lauren and olivia) and brad accents (lauren), MM kids trims (kate), vintage hip trims (paisley) and trinket pins, shadow box and sticky squares: Making Memories

Other: silk flower

PAGE 27 HILLARY LANDON

OLIVER

1. Choose photos and vintage hip papers and cut down to size of metal frames
2. Punch holes in corners of each photo and use scrapbook stitches to sew around each frame
3. Embellish each frame with buttons, leather label holders, painted gameboard shapes, painted metal mesh, stitched tin tiles, gameboard alphabet, fabric alphabet and leather frame
4. Place three embellished frames on each length of ribbon
5. Tie ribbons to a wooden dowel and tie knot at end of each ribbon
6. Trim ribbons and hang your project on the wall

Fabric alphabet (sophia), gameboard alphabet (lexi), gameboard shapes, leather frame, leather label holders, metal frames, metal mesh, scrapbook stitches, scrapbook colors acrylic paint (sherbet and hampton), stitched tin tiles, vintage hip buttons (gracen and paisley), paper (gracen) and trims (paisley): Making Memories

PAGE 28 GAIL PIERCE-WATNE

PHOTO WREATH

1. Print photos (about six) approximately 2½" x 2½" in size
2. Cut background piece of paper for each photo
3. Mount photos
4. Cut frame for each photo with a contrasting paper (the opening slightly smaller than the photo) and adhere
5. Punch hole in top of each frame
6. Thread ribbon through hole and tie on wreath

Vintage hip paper and trims: Making Memories

Other: wreath

PAGE 29 MELLETTE BEREZOSKI

PHOTO CANDLE TRIO

1. Attach same-sized photos to chipboard
2. Glue flat parts (heads) of four thumbtacks to back corners of each photo
3. Glue flat parts (heads) of two thumbtacks to each petite signage
4. Press photos and signage into candles
5. Add flower and gem sticker to one signage
6. Apply rub-ons alphabet to metal tray

Petite signage (journey), gem sticker and rub-ons alphabet (providence): Making Memories

Candles and metal tray: Compass Home, Inc.

Thumbtacks: A & W Products Co.

PAGE 30 LYNNE MONTGOMERY

GOALS 2006

1. To create box, you'll need two 5" x 5" stretched canvases, one serving as the front of box and the other as the back
2. Paint both sides of your canvas with acrylic paint including wooden inset on back and let dry
3. Hinge canvases together so they open like a book
4. Hot glue two long ribbons that will eventually be used to tie box closed
5. Glue ribbon around edge of each canvas, securing on bottom
6. Trim two pieces of patterned paper for inside portion of box, cut an opening in center and adhere to canvases
7. Embellish insides and outsides with your favorite photos and embellishments

Simply fabulous paper and trims (brooke), blossoms, mini brads, charmed frame, rub-ons, cardstock tag, safety pin, label holder, scrapbook colors acrylic paint, tag maker and tag maker rims: Making Memories

Silver handle: 7 Gypsies

Creative edge canvases: Fredrix

Hinges and screws (Stanley): Home Depot

Drapery clips: Umbra Inc.

Other: ribbon (gingham), twill tape and slide holder

PAGE 31 GAIL PIERCE-WATNE

HANGING FRAMES

1. Choose three soft metal frames like vintage hip and drill hole at top of frame about ⅜" across
2. Cut three pieces of ribbon in 9" lengths and fold in thirds
3. Cut a length of ribbon about 20" long, fold it at the 8" mark and push through drill hole just enough to create an opening
4. Slip folded ribbon through opening to create a bow
5. Tighten long ribbon around bow
6. Repeat steps with remaining two frames, leaving equal space between them

Vintage hip frames and trims: Making Memories

PAGE 32 LYNNE MONTGOMERY

SISTERS

1. Cut sheet metal to desired size, drill holes for hanging and clean with a de-greaser before starting
2. Paint entire surface (front and back) with a light solid color
3. Section off metal with painters tape and use a dark solid color to fill in untaped area
4. Age frame with brown paint and brown/black inks, then seal
5. Glue magnets to backs of buttons
6. Reinforce letters with chipboard backing, ink edges and glue magnets to back
7. Matte photo in coordinating paper, attach to frame with magnets and thread ribbon through holes for hanging

Vintage hip paper, buttons and trims, scrapbook colors acrylic paint kit, creative letters (wooden tiles) and distressing kit: Making Memories

Spray paint (shell white satin): Rust-Oleum Corporation

Super surface sealer: Design Master

Other: 16 gauge sheet metal, chipboard, de-greaser cleaner, magnets and painter's tape

PAGE 33 MELLETTE BEREZOSKI

GLASS PHOTO COASTERS

1. Attach photos to back of each sheer frame, covering only the windowed portion
2. Adhere a 3¼" x 3¼" piece of colored cardstock behind each photo
3. Add alphabet sticker for each person's initial to front of frame
4. Have pieces of glass cut to 3¼" x 3¼" and sand edges
5. Attach glass to top of each sheer frame by applying adhesive to corners
6. Add plastic bumpers to back of each coaster to prevent scratching surfaces

Sheer frames, all about alphas stickers and cardstock: Making Memories

Adhesive: E6000, Eclectic Products, Inc.

Plastic bumpers: Waxman

PAGE 36 MAGGIE HOLMES

MONOGRAM MIRROR

1. Resize and print photo to fit in smaller frame
2. Cut patterned paper to fit in other two frames
3. Cover metal monogram with white embossing ink and heat emboss
4. Once dry, paint monogram with iridescent glitter paint
5. Layer Making Memories' fabric flowers with a silk flower and adhere to middle frame
6. Adhere small photo and monogram to frame
7. Attach all three frames to front of mirror with double-sided tape

Patterned paper, metal monogram, flowers and rhinestone brads: Making Memories

Other: silk flowers, frames, mirror and paint

PAGE 37 LONI STEVENS

HISTORY

1. Mask off areas to create horizontal stripes with low-tack tape
2. Paint each section one at a time, letting paint dry before starting on next area
3. Adhere ribbon to canvas with double sided tape
4. Add sentiment to green stripe with rub-ons
5. Adhere silk flower with epoxy cement glue to secure
6. Add decorative push-pins through ribbon along left side rim

Ribbon, push-pins, scrapbook colors acrylic paint (poppy) and simply stated rub-ons: Making Memories

Acrylic paint (brown and green): Americana, DecoArt

Other: vintage trim

PAGE 38 ERIN TERRELL

MIRROR WITH QUOTE

1. Clean mirror surface completely and allow to dry
2. Measure 2" down from top of beveled edge of mirror and mark a line using a soft-tipped pencil
3. Apply Hudson and Misunderstood rub-ons to spell out quote
4. Draw a new line every 1½" down for next line of quote
5. Use Beach rub-ons to spell out author of quote and place 1" below previous line
6. Use a soft cloth to wipe away pencil marks or stray fingerprints
7. If mistakes are made while applying rub-ons, use a straight-edged razor to remove letters

Rub-ons alphabet (hudson, misunderstood and beach): Making Memories

Mirror: Pottery Barn

Other: cloth, ruler and soft-tipped pencil

PAGE 39 GAIL PIERCE-WATNE

BOHO LOVE

1. Select chipboard 8" letters
2. Apply Mod Podge to front of letter
3. Immediately place patterned paper on top of letter, patterned side up
4. When dry, cut around edge of each letter with a utility knife
5. Use sanding block to smooth out edges of chipboard and paper
6. Embellish with matching trim and brads
7. Tie on photos

Chipboard letters, boho chic paper, trims and brads (lauren) and gem stickers: Making Memories

PAGE 40 LONI STEVENS

PHOTO CLOCK

1. Cut a ¾" thick piece of wood down to an 8⁷⁄₁₆" x 8⁷⁄₁₆" square
2. Follow manufacturer's instructions while spraying several layers of home décor stain over tin frames and wood mounting block
3. Let each layer of spray dry before next application
4. Add photos to frames and adhere tins to wood block
5. Drill hole through wood and tin where inner corners of frames meet
6. Insert clock through hole and secure with clock hands

Vintage hip frames: Making Memories

Home décor stain sprays: Design Master

Other: adhesive and clock parts

PAGE 41 KRIS STANGER

MAGNETIC FRAME

1. Paint unfinished wood frame and let dry
2. Cover raised portion of frame with strips of paper
3. Apply thin layer of Mod Podge over paper area only
4. Once dry, rub entire surface with wax
5. Cut an 8" x 10" piece of steel, glue an 8" x 10" piece of solid paper to surface of steel and slightly distress with sand paper

6. Spray paint large Making Memories' magnetic clips with cream spray paint, let dry and glue on buttons and rhinestones
7. Glue flat magnets to backs of Making Memories' vintage buttons
8. Attach embellishments to frame

Scrapbook colors acrylic paint (manilla), vintage hip buttons and paper, large magnetic clips, rhinestone and pearl stickers: Making Memories

Wax: Minwax

Spray paint (cream): Krylon

Other: unfinished wood frame, steel and Plaid Mod Podge

PAGE 42 JENNIFER JENSEN

EVERYTHING HOOKS

1. Using a 2" x 4" or other piece of thick wood, cut three 4¼" x 4¼" squares of wood
2. Sand all rough edges and paint back and sides of all three wood squares
3. Trace wood size onto paper, trims and glue on top of wood
4. Seal paper and wood
5. Paint over frame, rubbing excess paint off to distress and adhere to top of wood square
6. Spray paint hooks all the same color
7. Mark placement of hook in center of frame and screw hooks into wood

Boho chic paper, gem stickers, scrapbook colors acrylic paint and vintage hip frames: Making Memories

Antique white spray paint: Krylon

Hooks: Target

Finishing wax: Minwax

PAGE 43 KRIS STANGER

MONOGRAM DOOR HANGER

1. Paint wooden plaque and let dry
2. Apply monogram sticker and layer of Mod Podge gloss lustre
3. Let dry
4. Drill two small holes at top of plaque for ribbon
5. Attach rhinestone brad accent to paper flower and glue to plaque

Scrapbook colors acrylic paint (manilla and rose petal), simply fabulous monogram alphabet stickers and trims (brooke), paper flowers and rhinestone brads: Making Memories

PAGE 46 JAYME SHEPHERD

PHOTO TRAY

1. Cut background paper and adhere to bottom of wood tray
2. Cut strips of ribbon and adhere to background paper
3. Adhere photo to center of tray and cut corners of vintage hip frame to create photo corners
4. Cover metal letters with Mod Podge or other adhesive and apply glitter
5. Add letters to bottom of photo
6. Add chipboard letter to photo and cover design with acrylic piece
7. Tie ribbon around outside of photo tray

Photo tray, boho chic paper (lauren), simply fabulous trims (brooke and meg), MM kids trims (kate), ribbon for cards, vintage hip (paisley), flower frame and buttons (paisley) and sticky squares: Making Memories

Chipboard letter: Lil' Davis Designs

Glitter: Art Glitter

Ribbon: Offray

PAGE 47 LONI STEVENS

LET THE JOURNEY BEGIN

1. Cover metal tin box entirely with hole re-enforcer stickers and paint over stickers
2. Let dry
3. Remove re-enforcers
4. Adhere signage to front of tin

Signage (life), scrapbook colors acrylic paint and mini brads: Making Memories

Hole re-enforcers: Staples

Tin lunchbox: Provo Craft

PAGE 48 MARGIE ROMNEY-ASLETT

RIBBON LAMP SHADE

1. Pick several types of ribbons and trims
2. Cut ribbons different lengths and use different end angles including french cut
3. Knot some of the ends
4. Adhere ribbons to top edge of a simple white cotton lampshade
5. Overlap ribbons, covering entire lampshade
6. Cover raw edges at top of lampshade by adhering a ribbon horizontally around rim

Cosmo ribbons, woven ribbons, MM kids trims (flower and ric rac), vintage hip trims (gracen), simply fabulous trims (green velvet), boho chic trims (brown gathered grosgrain) and ribbon glue: Making Memories

Other: May Arts ribbon

PAGE 49 LYNNE MONTGOMERY

BRAD EMBELLISHED CANDLES

1. Print out a spreadsheet with ½" size square boxes covering entire page
2. Cut paper to size so it is the same height as candle and will wrap one time around
3. Use an Anywhere Punch to make 1/16" holes in paper where lines from spreadsheet intersect, forming a pattern
4. Wrap paper around candle and fasten with tape
5. Stick brads through punched holes in paper, inserting them ¾ of the way in
6. When all brads have been placed, carefully tear away paper and push the rest of the way in

Anywhere punch, decorative brads, medium brads and mini brads: Making Memories

Other: candles

PAGE 50 AUDRE MATHIS

RED VH CANDLES

1. Glue paper on metal tags, sand edges and decorate with rub-ons
2. Use thin ribbons to tie tags onto large ribbon and glue around tallest candle
3. Add additional ribbons to all candles, gluing some and tying others
4. Place finishing touches by adding trinket pins, buttons and other small embellishments to ribbons
5. Adhere coordinating paper to cover box lid, creating candle stand

Vintage hip paper, trims, buttons and trinkets, tag shape eyelet charms, rub-ons images (love) and sand paper: Making Memories

Other: Plaid Mod Podge

PAGE 51 JENNIFER JENSEN

FRAMED BUTTON CLOCK

1. Remove glass from photo frame
2. Trace shape of bottom wood piece onto selected paper
3. Trim paper and adhere to wood piece
4. Seal paper
5. Mark center of paper and drill hole for clock mechanism and place clock hands
6. Mark twelve spots for button numbers (remember, the frame covers outer edge of paper-covered wood piece)
7. Glue buttons onto front of clock base
8. Place clock mechanism into drilled hole and assemble

Vintage hip buttons, boho chic paper (tweed) and simply fabulous gem stickers: Making Memories

Clock mechanism and clock hands: Walnut Hollow

Sealer: Minwax Finishing Wax

Other: picture frame

PAGE 52 LONI STEVENS

CHERISH ALL YOUR HAPPY MOMENTS

1. Type out quote in Photoshop and reverse text
2. Print onto an ink-jet transfer sheet
3. Transfer quote onto a long strip of white fabric with iron (follow manufacturer's instructions)
4. Cut two 14" x 14" squares of fabric for pillow
5. Machine stitch white fabric with quote onto front piece of pillow (before stitching the pillow pieces together)
6. Adhere ribbon with iron-on adhesives
7. Dye white flower aqua and set into fabric with decorative brads
8. Stitch pillow together

Petal (spotlight mix), decorative brads and boho chic trims (lauren): Making Memories

Computer font: ParmaPetit and QuickType

PAGE 53 LYNNE MONTGOMERY

FRAMED PHOTO COASTERS

1. Have pieces of glass cut into 4" x 4" squares, one piece for each coaster (cut glass will be a bit smaller than the overall size of vintage hip frames that will be used)
2. Add two additional strips of foam tape to backside of vintage hip frame, forming a square
3. After cleaning a square of glass, center it on backside and adhere to frame
4. Create a small photo collage to be viewed through frame's opening using various papers, clear defined stickers and rub-ons
5. Place a glue dot on front side of mini collage in each corner, center and hold frame over it and lay flat, adhering glue dots to glass
6. Cut a 4" x 4" square of black cardstock and adhere to back of glass, finishing off backside with photo tape
7. If you'd like, place a small felt pad on backside of each of the four corners

Cardstock (black), clear defined stickers, rub-ons mini, vintage hip frame and papers: Making Memories

Felt pads: Shepherd Hardware Products

Mini glue dots: Glue Dots International

Photo tape: 3L Corp

Other: foam tape, glass and old book paper

PAGES 54 – 55 MELLETTE BEREZOSKI

DECORATIVE BALLS TRIO

1. Paint unfinished balls and let dry
2. Brush on coat of clear, glossy sealer and let dry
3. Remove prongs from brads and hot glue to first ball
4. Apply rub-ons alphabet to second ball
5. Apply antiquing spray to a few white blossoms and let dry
6. Glue a mixture of green and antiqued blossoms across center of third ball
7. Apply page pebbles to small photos and attach to flower centers

Scrapbook colors acrylic paint, blossoms, page pebbles, medium metallic brads and rub-ons alphabet (circus): Making Memories

Antiquing spray: Krylon

Other: Plaid Mod Podge

GREETINGS CARD HOLDER

1. Remove desired monogram alphabet from sticker sheet, adhere to white cardstock for stability and cut out
2. Use a few letters as templates and cut out from photos
3. Apply Diamond Glaze to monogram alphabet and let dry completely (do not apply to photo letters)
4. Have a sheet of acrylic or plexiglass cut to 16" x 2" at a hardware or home improvement store
5. Drill six small holes close to top and bottom edges of acrylic strip and two small holes at left and right ends of strip (for hanging)
6. Attach circle clips to top and bottom edges of acrylic by threading wire through small holes and twisting in back
7. Attach monogram alphabets and photo letters to acrylic strip

Simply fabulous monogram alphabet stickers (brooke), silver circle clips and wire: Making Memories

Other: Judi-Kins Diamond Glaze

PAGE 56 LONI STEVENS

EVERYTHING GROWS WITH LOVE

1. Using low-tack tape, mask off rectangular shape on vase (use tape to cover all other areas you do not want sprayed)
2. Apply self-adhesive magic mesh over rectangular opening to create polka dot pattern

3. Following manufacturer's instructions for frosted glass spray, apply over area you want frosted and let dry
4. Remove mesh and low-tack tape to expose pattern on glass
5. Add rub-on sentiment over pattern
6. Drop marbles inside vase

Simply stated rub-ons, simply fabulous trims and buckle: Making Memories

Frosted glass spray: Rust-Oleum Corporation

Other: marbles

PAGE 57 KRIS STANGER

DISTRESSED CANDLE HOLDER

1. Start with a 4" x 4" x 12" block of wood and use router to make three 2¼" holes in top
2. Paint solid black and let dry
3. Stamp with decorative foam stamps, using manilla paint and let dry
4. Sand edges of holder as well as surface of stamped area
5. Apply brown antique gel over entire surface
6. Snip backs off decorative antique copper brads, arrange in diamond pattern and glue in place on front of holder
7. Add candles

Scrapbook colors acrylic paint (black and manilla), antique copper brads and foam stamps: Making Memories

Candles: Provo Craft

Gel wood stain (maple): Delta

PAGE 60 MELLETTE BEREZOSKI

WISHING JARS

1. Tie ribbons to neck of jars and secure by attaching photos
2. Fold 3" x 6" pieces of patterned paper in half and leave for guests to write messages
3. Print wishes on back side of various patterned papers
4. Cut into strips and wrap tightly around pencil to coil
5. Place in jar for guests to take

Simply fabulous paper (brooke) and ribbon cards: Making Memories

Glass jars: Target

PAGE 61 GAIL PIERCE-WATNE

SHOWER INVITATION

1. Using a computer, create invitation with colors the bride has selected for the wedding
2. Embellish with ribbon and secure using ribbon buckle
3. Select ribbon in different shades of predominate colors, measuring 1½" x 14"
4. If using wired ribbon, pull one of the wires out and gather ribbon by pulling second wire and twisting the base as you pull (if using non-wired ribbon, use a basting stitch along one edge and gather and turn as above)
5. Secure gathers with a few stitches at base
6. Add green ribbon for leaves
7. Set a few roses at each place setting for a shower favor or gather multiple roses together as a practice bouquet for the bride

Velvet ribbon and ribbon buckle: Making Memories

Other ribbon: Michaels

PAGE 62 LONI STEVENS

DECORATIVE GLASSES

1. Mask off areas you don't want sprayed with low-tack tape
2. Adhere strips of low-tack tape vertically down center of glass to create stripes
3. With circle cutter, cut a large circle out of a clear window decal and place over glass to create large circle
4. Create a mask by punching holes in low-tack tape with a circle paddle punch
5. Apply frosting spray over exposed areas
6. Let dry and remove tape
7. Add sentiments and colored images to glass with rub-ons

Rub-ons images (beach and love), rub-ons wordage (wedding) and nothing but numbers stickers: Making Memories

Circle punch: Paddle Punch, Provo Craft

Clear window decal (for mask): Hammermill

Frosted glass spray: Rust-Oleum Specialty, Rust-Oleum Corporation

Other: low-tack painter's tape

PAGE 63 JENNIFER JENSEN

OUR FRIENDS, OUR GUESTS

1. Embellish front of guest book with family monogram
2. Place on top of stamped portion of book
3. Add label sticker under photo
4. Using letter stamps and rub-ons, create title
5. Place family photo and note on inside of book for guests to read
6. Embellish edge of book with three buttons

Boho chic ephemera stickers and trims, crystal brads, foam stamps and rub-ons wordage: Making Memories

Other: buttons and letter stamps

PAGES 64 - 65 JULIE TURNER

A CELEBRATION OF FAMILY - PLACE CARD

1. Select a special photo of each guest to use in place card frame
2. Wipe boho chic frame and decorative brads with white acrylic paint for a vintage look
3. Attach a ribbon hanger to frame using brads
4. Mount photo in frame and back with boho chic paper
5. Add journaling to back that tells photo's story
6. Tie a tag to front that tells photo's year
7. Hang from corner of a chair to use as place card

A CELEBRATION OF FAMILY - INVITATION

1. Piece together a selection of boho chic coordinated papers to create invitation base
2. Embellish with a piece of trim and two brads
3. Add a sentimental photo

Artisan labels, boho chic paper, frame, photo corners, trims, brads and stickers and scrapbook colors acrylic paint: Making Memories

PAGE 66 AUDRE MATHIS

IT'S A PARTY

1. Paint bottom of small tin to match selected decorative papers
2. Soak paper bits in water and collage with Mod Podge to top of tin
3. Use tag maker and corresponding papers to create small tag
4. Use rub-ons to adhere guest's name, then tie tag to favor with matching ribbons
5. Cut large tag shape out of colored cardstock

6. Decorate cardstock tag with ribbons, brads and calling card stickers
7. Spell out 'what, where, when and rsvp' with mini alpha stickers and hand write party information

Simply fabulous paper (maddi), trims (maddi) and calling cards (friendship), textured cardstock (polo club), scrapbook colors acrylic paint (polo club), crystal brads (clear circle), boho chic tiny alphas (in bloom), tag rims and rub-ons alphabet (heidi): Making Memories

Other: Altoid's gum tin and Plaid Mod Podge

PAGE 67 LONI STEVENS

JOIN US

1. Dip flower stamp in versa mark ink
2. Press flower stamp onto card to create patterned background
3. Pour embossing powder over flowers, shake excess powder off and heat set with an embossing gun
4. Create cover out of vellum
5. Set large eyelets and string ribbon through vellum cover to close
6. Add woven label 'join us' to cover

Foam stamp (flower), ribbon and woven label: Making Memories

Large eyelet: Prim-Dritz

Other: vellum

PAGES 68 - 71 MELLETTE BEREZOSKI

SWEET 16 PLACE SETTING

1. Attach one end of wide ribbon to two D rings
2. Loop other end of ribbon through rings to create napkin holder
3. Attach colorboard tag with jump ring
4. Add stickers to cup to personalize and coordinate with other pieces
5. Fold patterned paper in half to create place card
6. Add cardstock with guest's name, colorboard tag and number stickers

Simply fabulous paper and trims (maddi), value pack stickers, MM kids number stickers (spotlight), crystal brads and jump rings: Making Memories

Cup: Wal Mart

D rings: Michaels

Paper flower: Prima

SWEET 16 INVITATION

1. Trim off front of card with scallop-edged scissors
2. Add number stickers and colorboard tag to front of card
3. Apply rub-ons wordage to tag and add gem sticker and ribbon
4. Attach photo along inside, right edge of card
5. Computer print information on white cardstock and attach next to photo

Card pads (springtime), nothing but numbers stickers, colorboard stickers (memories), ribbon, gem stickers and rub-ons wordage: Making Memories

Computer font: Tokyo girl

Decorative edged scissors: Fiskars

SWEET 16 GUEST BOOK

1. Cut two pieces of patterned paper the same size and adhere along three edges to create pocket
2. Adhere photo along left or right edge of pocket
3. Punch circle from top edge of pocket and attach to book
4. Cut a piece of solid cardstock to fit inside pocket
5. Add ribbon and crystal brad to top of tag
6. Add flowers and gem stickers to pockets

Simply fabulous mini book and paper (maddi), ribbons, crystal brads, gameboard shapes (flower) and gem stickers: Making Memories

Circle punch: Marvy Uchida

Paper flower: Prima

FRIENDSHIP FAVOR BOXES

1. Paint box lids with spotlight paint (paint inside of boxes if desired)
2. Cut piece of patterned paper the same height as box and long enough to wrap around completely
3. Glue paper around box and apply sealer if desired
4. Attach photo to top of lid
5. Attach ribbon around sides of lid and cover seam with charmed enamel

Simply fabulous paper (maddi), avenue collection paper (coral), ribbon, scrapbook colors acrylic paint (spotlight) and charmed enamel (flowers): Making Memories

Other: papier-mâché boxes

PAGE 74 MAGGIE HOLMES

FILE FOLDERS PHOTO STORAGE

1. Resize and print photos to fit on folder's label tab
2. Cut a strip of patterned paper and a square of cardstock for each folder
3. Dry emboss circles on cardstock squares and create titles with letter stickers and rub-ons alphabet
4. Attach flowers with brads
5. Use sewing machine to stitch down both sides of each folder, creating pockets

Patterned paper, letter stickers, rub-ons alphabet and brads: Making Memories

Flowers: Prima

File folders and wire organizer: Office Supply Store

Other: sewing machine and staples

PAGE 75 MARGIE ROMNEY-ASLETT

SHADOW BOX

1. Find a great shadow box
2. Choose your photos
3. Cut printed paper and photos and adhere to backboard
4. Paint and sand jigsaw alphas
5. Embellish with cardstock tags, ribbon, chipboard and beads
6. Reassemble shadow box

Jigsaw alphabet, scrapbook colors acrylic paint, tiny alphas, cardstock tags, ribbon brads, MM kids trims (gingham), safety pin, blossoms, accent brads, chipboard tag, flowers, defined stickers and vintage hip paper (paisley): Making Memories

Shadow box: TJ Maxx

Printed paper (stripe): Chatterbox

Printed paper (flower): SEI

Ribbon: May Arts

Other: beads and shimmer

PAGE 76 GAIL PIERCE-WATNE

EMBELLISHMENT JARS

1. Select spice containers in a size and shape that fits your style
2. Spray paint both oval tag maker rims and spice jar lids in whichever color you choose
3. Cut out patterned or colored paper to coordinate with rims and lids and write or use rub-ons to indicate jar contents (this can also be done on the computer)
4. Put labels in tag maker rims and crimp

5. Punch small holes at each end of the labels, tie ribbon through one end, wrap around jar and tie
6. Use same ribbon to wrap around jar lid and secure with ribbon glue

Vintage hip paper, trims and tag maker rims: Making Memories

Spice jars: Target

PAGE 77 JAYME SHEPHERD

VINTAGE PAPER BOXES

1. For large box, tie velvet and lace trim around base tie in front and trim ends
2. Stick two decorative pins through ribbon knot
3. For small box, adhere lace around lid
4. Select photo for metal frame and adhere to box
5. Finish off metal frame by adding flower, pin and button embellishments

Vintage hip paper boxes, trims (gracen), buttons (paisley), trinket pins and frame (scallop): Making Memories

PAGE 78 SKYLAR NIELSEN

RIBBON RACK

1. Cut a piece of wooden molding approximately 2' long
2. Drill holes in molding with a ⅜" bit approximately 5" apart
3. Cut ⅜" wooden dowel approximately 12" long
4. Glue dowels in holes of molding
5. Paint and distress molding and dowels
6. Stack ribbon on dowels

Wooden molding and dowels: hardware store

Ribbon: Michaels

PAGE 79 GAIL PIERCE-WATNE

RIBBON JARS

1. Select glass vases large enough to hold a collection of ribbon (6" squares work well)
2. Divide ribbon into like colors
3. Select a ribbon from each color group that is the same width and pattern
4. Tie one around each vase and fill

Ribbon: Making Memories and Michaels

Other: glass vases

PAGE 80 JIHAE KWON

EMBELLISHED MOS

1. Divide space according to your needs and cut papers to size
2. Adhere papers on MOS board

3. Cover borders using various trims
4. Tie ribbons on container lids

Boho chic paper and trims: Making Memories

Other: glue dots and spray adhesive

PAGE 81 KRIS STANGER

PHOTO CD BOX

1. Make a pattern out of scratch paper (include a tab), trace onto decorative paper or scraps and cut out
2. Cut a square or rectangular piece (depending on size of divider) to go across back
3. Stitch down sides and around bottom using a straight stitch (use glue or brads to simplify)
4. For expandable dividers. fold two extra side pieces accordion style and glue in between front and back pieces
5. Incorporate paper used on dividers onto box, add a few embellishments and label

Boho chic paper and trims, vintage hip alphabet stickers, paper flowers, rhinestone stickers, petite signage, rhinestone brads and ribbon glue: Making Memories

Other: lime box

PAGES 82 - 83 ERIN TERRELL

SCRAPBOOK STORAGE SHELF

1. Purchase or locate a shelf
2. Clean shelf and add a few coats of Making Memories' spotlight paint
3. Use sandpaper from distressing kit to sand away paint on edges and roughen surfaces
4. Trim paper to fit shelves and use decoupage paste to adhere
5. If desired, add new doorknobs
6. Drill tiny holes for label holders and attach in place (for extra support, add wood glue in holes when brads are put in place)

Distressing kit, label holders (small rectangle, meadow), vintage hip paper (paisley) and scrapbook colors acrylic paint (spotlight): Making Memories

Other: Plaid Mod Podge (matte finish)

RIBBON CONTAINERS

1. Purchase 4 and 6 oz. tins from The Container Store
2. Trim Making Memories' ribbon to fit around tins (9" for 6 oz. and 7¼" for 4 oz.)
3. Use double sided tape or Making Memories' ribbon glue to attach ribbon to tins

Simply fabulous trims (brooke) and ribbon glue: Making Memories

Tins: The Container Store

PAGE 86 ERIN TERRELL

ART FRAMES

1. Locate your favorite photos from an art book (I chose photos from Making Memories' Creative Library)
2. Purchase standard-sized frames for art
3. Have custom mattes cut to fit the art and frame (this is very inexpensive)
4. Add titles to art by applying rub-ons to mattes

Rub-ons alphabet (circus and valentine) and creative library volume 1 (paint book): Making Memories
Frames and custom mattes: Hobby Lobby

PAGE 87 MELLETTE BEREZOSKI

PEN HOLDER BOOKENDS

1. Paint bookends with scrapbook colors paint
2. Add vintage hip border stickers to edges and center groove of bookends
3. Attach flower trim around middle of one potting tin
4. Attach base of tins to bookends

Scrapbook colors acrylic paint (shopping bag), vintage hip border stickers and trims (gracen): Making Memories
Potting tins: PromoSeeds Ltd.
Wooden bookends: Michaels

PAGE 88 SHERELLE CHRISTENSEN

SCRAP ROOM BOXES

1. Cut patterned papers to cover sides of boxes
2. Using a tape runner for simplicity or a decoupage medium for durability, adhere all pieces to sides of boxes
3. For boxes one and two, cut two different patterned papers to size of lid
4. Holding these two pieces together, cut from corner to corner, resulting in four of each piece
5. Using only two pieces of each color, create design on lid as shown
6. Cut strips to fit sides of lid and adhere
7. Add ric rac and other dimensional embellishments

Vintage hip paper, trims (gracen and paisley), findings, buttons and trinkets and petals: Making Memories
Papier-mâché box set: Heart and Home
Tim Holtz distress ink (antique linen): Ranger Industries
Other: chenille

PAGE 89 MARGIE ROMNEY-ASLETT

SHIMMERED ALPHA

1. Apply Mod Podge to front of alpha using a foam brush
2. Heavily sprinkle alpha with shimmer
3. Let dry completely
4. Tie woven ribbon as a simple embellishment

Woven ribbon: Making Memories
Other: dimensional alpha, glitter and Plaid Mod Podge

PAGE 90 LONI STEVENS

ART DOESN'T HAVE TO BE PERFECT

1. Paint entire 'A' with Making Memories' sky blue paint and let dry
2. Mask off edges with low-tack tape, paint center of 'A' with Making Memories' cornflower blue color and let dry
3. Keep tape over edges
4. Add letter stickers over monogram to add quote
5. Spray dark home décor stain over 'A' and let dry
6. Lift stickers to expose quote
7. Add graphic icons and star rub-ons

Scrapbook colors acrylic paint (cornflower and sky), all about alphas stickers, rub-ons images (snow) and simply stated rub-ons: Making Memories
Circle rub-ons: Pure Juice, Memories Complete
Rub-on graphic icons: KI Memories

PAGE 91 MAGGIE HOLMES

PERSONALIZED PAPER ORGANIZER

1. Resize and print two photos to fit in open spots of organizer
2. Apply rub-ons to photos and put in place
3. Cut a square of patterned paper to fit in third spot and use a square punch to create an opening
4. Adhere metal mesh behind opening and back with white cardstock
5. Attach sticker, flowers and rub-ons to square
6. Adhere ribbon and jelly label to front of organizer

Patterned paper, sticker, blossoms, rub-ons, metal mesh, ribbon, jelly label and rhinestone brads: Making Memories
Flower: Prima

PAGE 92 LYNNE MONTGOMERY

WHITE LAMP

1. Decide how many petal groupings you will need
2. Fasten petal groupings together with brads (using decorative brads for larger petals and mini brads for smaller petals)
3. Using a glue gun, adhere petals to bottom edge of lamp shade

Decorative brads, mini brads and petals: Making Memories
Other: glue gun and lampshade

PAGE 93 KRIS STANGER

HANGING BUCKET

1. Paint entire surface of bucket with celery paint and let dry
2. Gently brush manilla paint over raised section of bucket, creating additional dimension
3. Cut paper using scallop-edged scissors to cover top and bottom section of bucket and glue to attach
4. Apply Mod Podge to entire surface area of bucket covered by paper or paint and let dry
5. Optional: attach Making Memories' magnetic clips for labeling or further embellishment

Boho chic paper, magnetic clips, scrapbook colors acrylic paint (celery and manilla) and label tag: Making Memories
Bucket: Michaels
Other: Plaid Mod Podge

PAGE 94 JULIE TURNER

JILLIAN'S WORLD

1. Spray paint tag rims with a coordinating color
2. Using tag template, trace and cut patterned paper, transparency film and photos to fill all tags (since the project is viewed from both sides, each tag will need two pieces to create a front and back)
3. Insert tag pieces into rims and crimp closed with tag maker tool
4. Decorate tags with stickers and gems
5. Use a needle to punch holes in top and bottom of each tag and string together with invisible thread
6. Hang from ceiling with small eye screws
7. Touch up any paint chips on rim by spraying a puddle of paint into a disposable cup and dab onto chip with a small makeup sponge

Gem stickers, simply fabulous paper, sticker and seal pad, tag maker rims and tag maker: Making Memories
Invisible thread: Grilon
Spray paint: Krylon
Transparency film: 3M

PAGE 95 ERIN TERRELL

SWEET TREATS

1. Clean exterior of dish and allow to dry
2. Add rub-ons to outside of dish
3. Hand wash as needed

Rub-ons alphabet (ransom): Making Memories

Other: candy dish and soft cloth for cleaning

PAGE 96 ERIN TERRELL

PHOTO CUBE

1. Print photos large enough to cover papier-mâché box, sand edges and adhere
2. Cover leftover areas of box with decorative paper, sand edges and adhere
3. Add paper to chipboard shapes, sand edges and add decorative flowers
4. Trim flower from a sheet of KI Memories paper, spray paint white and adhere, trimming away excess
5. Add rhinestones to centers of all flowers
6. Use rub-ons to add quote along lid (box is turned upside-down)
7. Create and store 6" x 6" mini albums inside box

Chipboard shapes (circles, squares and rectangles), distressing kit sandpaper, gem stickers, label holder (cranberry), rub-ons mini (remember), rub-ons alphabet (heidi and hudson), vintage hip buttons, findings (gracen) and paper (paisley and gracen) and 6" x 6" album (kraft cover and inserts): Making Memories

Glue dots: Glue Dots International

Ghost shape silhouettes (daisies): Heidi Swapp

Patterned paper (large flower): KI Memories

Spray paint (white): Krylon

Papier-mâché box: Hobby Lobby

PAGE 97 MAGGIE HOLMES

MESSAGE BOARD

1. Cut strips of ribbon to size and adhere to chalkboard
2. Write quote with various letter stickers
3. Create calendar in Photoshop and print on cardstock
4. Resize photo to same size as calendar and print

Ribbon, letter stickers, chalkboard, bulldog clips and ribbon slide: Making Memories

Fonts: Scoutlight DB, Bebas, Fabianestem and Times

Other: rhinestone

PAGE 100 JAYME SHEPHERD

ABC CHILDREN'S ROOM BORDER

1. Trace letters onto selected paper and cut
2. Adhere paper cut-out to wooden letters using Mod Podge
3. Sand edges of each wooden letter
4. Add picture to each letter
5. Embellish letters with ribbon, rub-ons, buttons and pins

Decorative wood letters, boho chic paper and trims (lauren), MM kids paper (ethan and max), vintage hip buttons (gracen) and trinkets (pins), gameboard shapes, charmed (baby) and rub-ons (baby): Making Memories

Other: Plaid Mod Podge and Basic Grey rub-ons

PAGE 101 KRIS STANGER

BUCKETS OF FUN

1. Paint buckets and let dry
2. Apply Mod Podge and let dry
3. Attach trims by both gluing and knotting
4. Add stickers and carefully glue down corners with small dot of superglue
5. Fill buckets

MM kids stickers, trims and tags (kate and ethan) and scrapbook colors acrylic paint (waterslide and rose petal): Making Memories

Buckets: Michaels

Other: superglue, jute and Plaid Mod Podge

PAGE 102 AUDRE MATHIS

KID'S DOOR HANGER

1. Spell your child's name with jigsaw alphas, using negative letter shapes as a frame for photos or corresponding papers
2. Cover each letter with decorative papers or paint
3. Embellish covered letters with ribbons, buttons, staples and string
4. Glue letters together and insert photos
5. Glue matching ribbon to back of piece so it can be hung around a doorknob or wall hook
6. Re-enforce back with book binding tape (optional)

MM kids paper and trims (emma and max) and buttons, scrapbook colors acrylic paint (childhood), jigsaw alphabet (poolside), stitches (primary orange), colored staples and book binding tape: Making Memories

PAGE 103 MAGGIE HOLMES

ART DISPLAY

1. Resize and print photos to cover entire magnet board
2. Cut strips of patterned paper to create border on wooden portion of frame
3. Paint chipboard letters and adhere to border
4. Adhere rhinestones to some of the letters
5. Use magnetic bulldog clips on board for art work display

Patterned paper, chipboard letters, scrapbook colors acrylic paint and bulldog clips: Making Memories

Other: rhinestones and magnet board

PAGE 104 SHERELLE CHRISTENSEN

HANGING PHOTO FRAMES

1. Cut three square pieces of chipboard
2. Cover each piece with a patterned paper, cut to exact size
3. Ink and sand around edges for distressed look
4. Punch holes in top and bottom of top two pieces and top of third piece
5. Lace ribbon through holes to connect pieces
6. Add photos, embellishments and journaling to complete project

MM kids paper, button and decorative pin, simply fabulous paper and decorative pin, vintage hip trims and buttons and crystal brads: Making Memories

PAGE 105 KRIS STANGER

CHILDREN'S PATCHWORK STOOL

1. Cut and arrange papers
2. After placing paper, stitch around border of a few pieces using a sewing machine and glue down
3. Add rub-ons, apply a layer of Mod Podge, let dry and repeat
4. Add petite signage and a gemstone sticker to center of flower
5. Glue velvet ribbon to base of stool using ribbon glue

Velvet trims, ribbon glue, boho chic paper, gemstone stickers, rub-ons and rhinestone ribbon charm: Making Memories

Other: Plaid Mod Podge

Pre-painted stool: Joanne Crafts

PAGE 106 JENNIFER JENSEN

KIDS PENDANT PILLOW

1. Cut front and back of team jersey to cover pillow form measurements, with an approximate 1" seam allowance
2. Print photo onto iron-on paper, trim into shape of number on back of shirt and iron-on photo over team number
3. Using foam stamps, add 'SCORE!' onto fabric and stitch around the 'C' and 'R'
4. Stitch soccer ribbon onto fabric and rub on simply stated words to embellish
5. Cut approximately fourteen 3-4" pieces of various coordinating ribbons and pin to both outer edges of jersey
6. Place the two cut pieces of jersey on top of one another with right sides together and pin to hold in place
7. Stitch around all sides, leaving a gap to turn right side out, and stuff pillow into fabric (do not leave opening on sides of pillow where ribbon fringe is located)

Foam stamps, scrapbook colors acrylic paint, simply stated rub-ons (sports) and woven ribbon (black and white): Making Memories

Other: soccer twill tape

Pillow form: Fairfield

PAGE 107 JENNIFER JENSEN

UP, UP, UP!

1. Cut a 5' piece of canvas with pinking shears for chart background and using a pencil, lightly mark placement for numbers and inch markings
2. Trace large number stickers and large stars onto fabric and cut out
3. Using foam stamps, make inch markings on edge of chart and adhere numbers and label holders marked 'feet' in between inch marks
4. Starting slightly above the '2', adhere large fabric star, button stars and stamped stars

5. Lightly trace swirl marks above and below star cluster and back stitch using a large eye needle and thin ribbon (tie extra ribbon pieces to stitches)
6. Rub on saying under and over stitched ribbon
7. Cut out square of canvas on chart with pinking shears and stitch two vinyl pieces behind open square, creating pocket for changeable photo

Brads, fabric (grace), foam stamps, label holders, MM kids buttons, nothing but numbers stickers, scrapbook colors acrylic paint, ribbon and rub-ons alphabet (mixed brite): Making Memories

Canvas fabric: Jo-Ann's Fabric

Other: dowel, buttons, mini ric rac and vinyl

PAGE 108 KRIS STANGER

KEEPSAKE FRAMES

1. Apply pink paint to baby's hand and foot and press onto white linen paper
2. Print out a black and white photograph onto white linen paper
3. Cut these three items to desired shape and put into frame
4. Staple velvet ribbon to back of frame

KNOBS

1. Spray paint wooden knobs with cream paint and let dry
2. Apply Mod Podge to paper flowers, let dry and add rhinestone brads
3. Glue dry flowers to top of wooden knobs
4. Screw knobs to wall and hang frame from ribbon

Vintage hip trims (velvet ribbon), scrapbook colors acrylic paint (rose petal), linen paper, paper flowers, rhinestone brads and rub-ons mini (baby): Making Memories

Cream spray paint: Krylon

Other: frames, unfinished wooden knobs and Plaid Mod Podge

PAGE 109 MELLETTE BEREZOSKI

WEEKDAY PHOTO HANGERS

1. Cut a piece of patterned paper the size of hanger front
2. Adhere paper to hanger and coat with clear sealer
3. Place photo in frame and attach to hanger with foam tape
4. Tie ribbon around top of hanger
5. Add eyelet to corner of gameboard alphabet and attach to ribbon with safety pin

Vintage hip paper and frames, ribbon, gameboard alphabet (lexi), eyelets and safety pins: Making Memories

Hangers: Ikea

Other: Plaid Mod Podge

PAGE 110 MARGIE ROMNEY-ASLETT

ALTERED MOS

1. Pick a theme or color scheme
2. Foam stamp your child's name around MOS cloth canvas board
3. Cut an old pair of jeans into strips, then fray edges
4. Adhere jean strips around edge of MOS board with fabric glue
5. Add favorite photos and memos

MOS cloth canvas board, scrapbook colors acrylic paint (navy, eat your carrots and cornflower) and foam stamps (jersey, uppercase and star form basic shapes): Making Memories

Other: old pair of jeans

PAGE 111 ELENI KARAHALIOS

RIBBON WREATH

1. Use a Styrofoam form measuring 12" x 2"
2. Cut approximately 50 lengths of ribbon, 25" long (use 3 widths – 1", ⅞" and ⅜")
3. Tie ribbon in bows around form, starting with widest, at various intervals
4. Tie the next widest ribbon
5. Finish with the narrowest

Polka dot ribbon: The Lace Place

Styrofoam form: Michaels

MELLETTE BEREZOSKI
CROSBY, TEXAS

Mellette is a stay-at-home mom and reality-TV junkie who admits that she's a messy scrapbooker but likes to clean up in-between projects. When not working on an assignment, you'll most likely find her on her back porch browsing through mail order catalogs, flipping through her old book collection or admiring her flower garden.

LYNNE MONTGOMERY
GILBERT, ARIZONA

Lynne's most recent accomplishment is that she ran in her first 10 mile race. And she had plenty of time to train since she hasn't watched television in the last five years. She is an avid collector of hair magazines, loves homemade blackberry pie and can hardly buy anything without a coupon.

MAGGIE HOLMES
SOUTH JORDAN, UTAH

Even though she's the mother of three boys, Maggie is all girl. A self-confessed fashionista, she's currently working on expanding her growing collection of purses and bags. Always cheerful, smiling and organized, the one thing she'd have if she were stranded on a desert island would be TiVO.

KRIS STANGER
ST. GEORGE, UTAH

To Kris, there's nothing finer than a good pedicure and manicure. Since she's the mother of four, including a newborn, a little pampering is just what she deserves. Other loves include Bath and Body Concentrated Room Spray, planting flowers in the spring, Oprah and the color green in every shade.

JENNIFER JENSEN
HURRICANE, UTAH

A self-described Coke-only drinker (no diet!), Jennifer is terrified of snakes, mice and heights. But that doesn't stop her from doing the things she loves – trailer camping, cooking and baking, eating eggs for breakfast, exercising and talking on the phone for hours.

LONI STEVENS
PLEASANT GROVE, UTAH

You'll rarely find Loni without a Diet Dr. Pepper in her hand and good tunes playing in the background. Born on the day Mount St. Helen's erupted in 1980, she's a devoted family gal whose childhood dream was to be a makeup artist/hair stylist to the stars.

ERIN TERRELL
SAN ANTONIO, TEXAS

Originally from South Carolina, Erin confesses that her least favorite household chore is cleaning up her scrapbook room. She'd much rather be enjoying the spring weather, reading InStyle magazine, grilling outside, traveling or taking landscape photography.

JULIE TURNER
GILBERT, ARIZONA

The Château de l'Isle-Marie in France and the Hotel Del Coronado in California. Just a couple of the interesting places in Julie Turner's "collection" of interesting places to stay. When not traveling to exotic locales, she manages to stay busy home schooling her three children, working on projects and remodeling her house.

CREATIVE DIRECTOR OF PUBLICATIONS
GAIL PIERCE-WATNE
MURRAY, UTAH

Although relatively new to the scrapbooking industry, Gail Pierce-Watne is no amateur in the world of design. Her longtime passion began when she designed the bulletin boards for her first grade class. She believes her greatest talent in life, next to her near-perfect impersonation of Shania Twain, is raising an outstanding family.

CONTRIBUTING ARTISTS

JOANNA BOLICK
FLETCHER, NORTH CAROLINA

SHERELLE CHRISTENSEN
SHELLEY, IDAHO

be inspired.™